A Sea Story

A Book on Death and Dying

Written By Kore RavenSea
Illustrated By Aeowyn Riverwood

1st Edition

ISBN 978-1-936922-97-0
Edited by Luna Hoagland-Gallacher
Front Cover Illustrations by Aeowyn Riverwood
Cover Design by Aeowyn Riverwood
Book Design by Luna Hoagland-Gallacher

Printed and bound in the USA

Published by:
Pendraig Publishing Inc
PO Box 8427
Green Valley Lake, CA 92341

www.pendraigpublishing.com

For my beautiful son,
Dylan.

"Mama, what happens when we die?"

"Sit in my lap, dear one,
and I'll tell you all that I know."

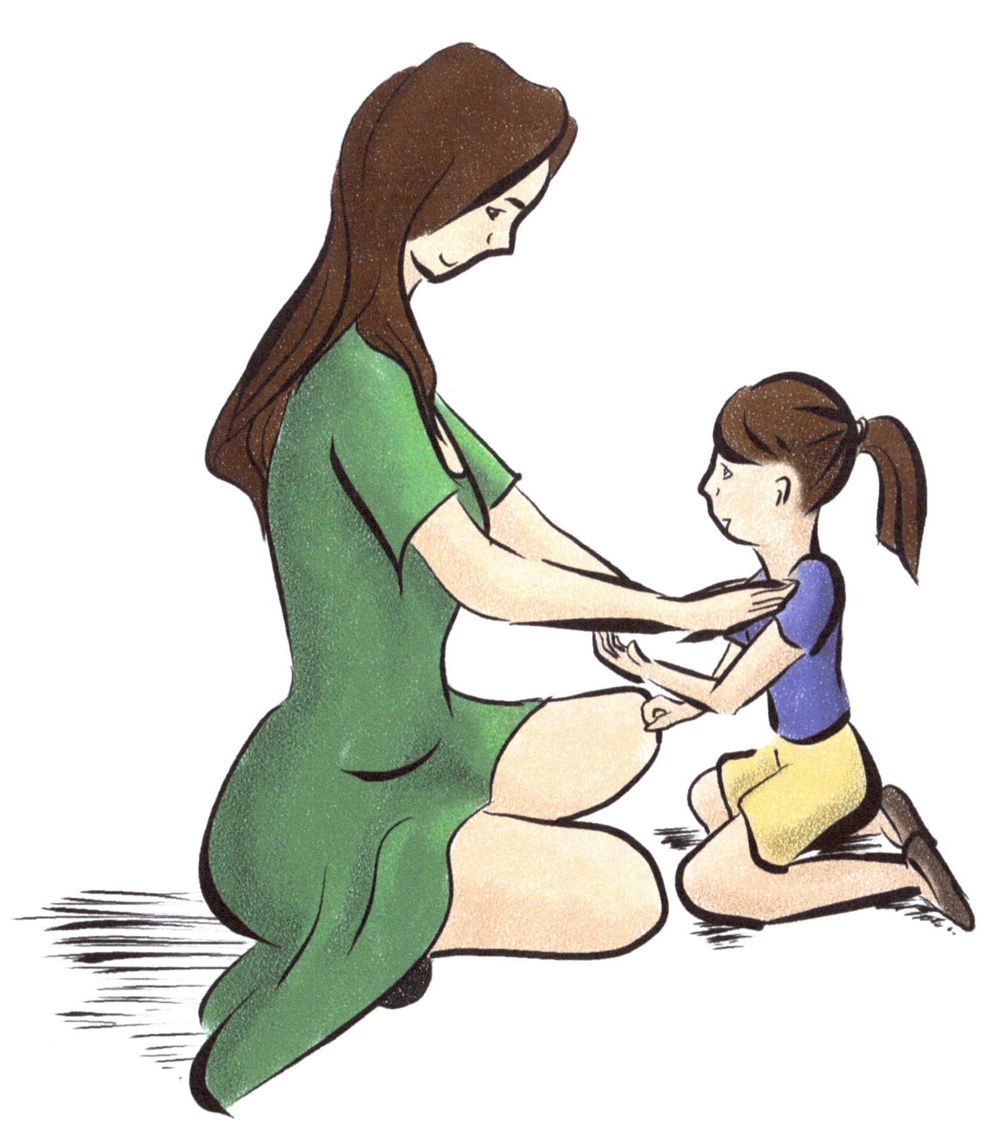

"When we die, our souls leave our bodies."
"What is a soul?"

"A soul is the part of you that makes you Willow and not Rowan."
"Our souls leave our bodies and travel elsewhere.
Some say that we travel to a far away place where there is endless candy, and cookies, and ice cream, and happiness."

"I would love to go there, Mama."
"We all would, dear one."

"Some say that our soul leaves our body and then nothing else happens. It's peaceful and quiet forever and ever."

"Like when I go to sleep at night?"

"Exactly."

"Others say that we are reborn again, into
different people, in a different time.
This is called reincarnation."
"Reincarnation. What are we born as, mama?"

"Well, some say we are reborn as people. As someone else all-together. As Olive, instead of Tobias. Some say we are born as someone else, but we can remember who we were before."

"Can we be born as a dog, like Sara?"
"Yes, in fact, some people say we are reborn as people, and even plants, like the flowers beneath your beautiful feet."

"Why do we die, mama?"

"Well, I'll describe it to you this way, my dear one: Life is like the ocean. Do you remember when we went to the beach last summer with grandma and grandpa?"

"Yes."

"Life is like the ocean. The waves
are endlessly flowing.
The tides come in and out.
They go through cycles, as we do in our lives.
We grow from little ones, like you, and
eventually become very old,
like grandma and grandpa.
The tides go in and out, and so do we,
with the changes of the Moon,
the Sun, the seasons.
Our whole world is like the ocean."

"But just like the tides must go in, our bodies get tired, and draw to an end. Do you remember that sunset we watched on the ocean?"
"Yes. The sun disappeared into the sea."

"That's right. The Sun went down, so the Moon can come up. It went under the sea, to sleep, to rest. That's just like people. For the world to keep growing, the old must die, so new people can be born."

"Is it scary to die, mama?"

"Witches like us, we believe that we go on to a place called the Summerlands. This is a beautiful place, where there are all your favorite things. We believe you stay in the Summerlands until you are reincarnated."

"So I will be happy and safe
until I am reborn again."
"That's right."

"Mama, can I talk to people that die?"
"Yes, in fact you can. Those that die are always with us in our hearts and in our memories. We can talk to them any time we want to. They are always listening."

"So grandma can hear me if I talk to her?"
"Yes. She can. Those that we love are never lost. They, in turn, will return to us."

"I'm sleepy, mama."

"Lay down your head, little one. Remember: Like the waves of the sea refresh and renew, so is the cycle of life and of death. Like the ocean, both life, and death are beautiful. We are all connected to each other and are connected in our hearts forever."

"I love you, mama."

"I love you always, in this life and beyond, dear one."

www.ingramcontent.com/pod-product-compliance
Lightning Source LLC
LaVergne TN
LVHW060635110826
845147LV00014B/911

9781936922970